AT CROSS PURPOSES

Handling Conflict in the Church

**Martin Eggleton
and
David Trafford**

CONTENTS

AT CROSS PURPOSES

Handling Conflict in the Church

INTRODUCTION

This is a 'how to' book. It is not intended to be theologically or analytically exhaustive. It does not set out to address all the philosophical issues around the nature of conflict. It suggests, as simply as possible, how conflict may be approached and dealt with, as well as offering material for study, prayer and reflection. It is written as a guide to those who may be asked, or who have particular professional responsibility to help Christians and churches handle the conflicts they inevitably face, but it is intended to be accessible to church members who want to do what they can to help when tensions and divisions occur in their own church. Devotional and reflective material and practical exercises have been placed alongside material describing the techniques and processes involved in peacemaking, to enable groups as well as individuals to consider the spiritual dimension of addressing conflict.

It is not written from the perspective of one Christian denomination, and it avoids commenting upon particular denominational structures. It aims to be as universal in its application as possible. Almost any organisational structure can be made to work where the will, the gifts and the necessary human qualities are present. No structure, however good, works without human co-operation, and though divinely inspired in its nature and inception, the Church cannot avoid being a human institution. So the resolution of conflict is not primarily about changing structures, though structural change may be one of the results of any process of conflict resolution. Whenever a structure is involved, and the family is one such structure, the place of people in that structure will be one aspect of the conflicts that arise within it.

So this book asks what elements are necessary if conflicts in churches are to have positive outcomes, and what kind of process conflict resolution is. The practical material about conflict resolution comes out of the work that David Trafford has been doing as a Pastoral Consultant in the Thames North Province of the United Reformed Church. In this he works as part of a team which offers pastoral and facilitational support to churches and ministers. The team includes a psychotherapist who is also a priest, working exclusively and confidentially with individuals, and three ministers in part-time pastoral ministries, who work with the Provincial Moderator, offering support and intervention in situations where it is needed. The devotions, Bible studies, and other material come out of Martin Eggleton's experience of Methodist ministry and chaplaincy work in ecumenical contexts.

The authors wish to express their thanks to the Methodist Church Pastoral Care Committee, who encouraged them to proceed with this project, and particularly to Ann Bird, who has inspired the whole Church to look seriously at the role of Pastoral Care in problematic situations.

CHAPTER ONE

THE NATURE OF CONFLICT

Conflict is a fact of life: we all live with it. Over 50 per cent of ministers and church leaders have had experience of major conflict in church life, according to a recent survey (P. Beasley-Murray, *Power for God's Sake*, Paternoster Press 1998). It is a necessary part of growth: every child comes into conflict with its parents/carers and other authority figures, because part of the child's learning is to discover the boundaries of acceptable behaviour, and no child is happy unless it is able to establish where those boundaries lie, and what sanctions will be applied when they are crossed. Conflict is no less a fact of life within the Church, and of any growth that is happening within it; a church without conflict is a dead church, a cosy corner for escapists.

We tend to see conflict in negative terms. Yet it is not negative in itself. Western systems of democratic government are based upon conflict between different political parties. Courts operate on an adversarial system in seeking justice, and football would have little crowd appeal if it lacked conflict! Most novels would be dull if they did not revolve around a situation of conflict. Conflict is an integral part of many processes, and is not in itself harmful. It only becomes harmful when it cannot be resolved, and when it becomes endemic, affecting the health of individuals, communities and systems of management. Like silence, conflict can have positive or negative meanings, and can be healing and constructive, or divisive and destructive.

This book is about how we can accept and respond positively to conflict in the context of the Church. It is based upon the premise that *it is the way that we respond to conflict* which determines whether the outcome of that conflict is creative and healthy, or limiting and unhealthy.

THE FORMS OF CONFLICT

Conflict takes many forms, and occurs at different levels of our experience. We all experience conflict within ourselves, as we have to choose between different things that we would like for ourselves, or for others. For instance, our enjoyment of food can come into conflict with our desire to be healthy and fit, and so we may limit our eating to those foods which are healthy, in quantities which are not excessive. Or we may decide that we are not concerned about our health, and are happy to eat what we like, when we feel like it. Conflict only arises when we are unable to balance or decide between the two factors, and then it can become a major source of discomfort and unhappiness in our lives as we alternately binge and diet.

Conflicts in churches happen between individuals. They may be simple clashes of personality, or they may be concerned with power, as when a church organist or worship leader clashes with the minister/vicar over who chooses the hymns/music. Sometimes individuals come to represent a point of view within their church, and may see themselves as the spokesperson for a particular group. This may bring them into conflict with others representing other points of view, though such clashes may not be personal at all. Interestingly, church treasurers apparently see more conflict in the church than other church officers do!

Conflicts arise between individuals and communities, where, for instance, a minister may wish to introduce a new hymn book to the church, and the congregation objects on the ground of cost or because a change in the musical culture of the church would result. Ministers are accused of failing to visit members of the congregation enough, or of exerting too much control in leadership teams, but more commonly it is the conduct of worship which produces the most criticism and conflict.

Conflicts also arise between groups within churches because people operate from within power bases; the catering staff is often such a power base, or the flower arrangers, the housegroup leaders or advice centre staff. Because people understand themselves as serving God from their particular positions, they will often fight ferociously to protect the tasks, the people and the organisation of their 'power base'.

There is sometimes conflict between churches, particularly over resources, and an obvious example is in a shared ministry, where one church feels that the other church is getting the greater share of the minister's time and energy. And conflicts occur within denominations as a whole, especially over matters of theology, authority and structure. An obvious example at the moment is the conflict occurring within most denominations over the theological and pastoral issues concerned with homosexual relationships.

CHRISTIANS AND CONFLICT

Is there anything unique about conflict in the Church, or is it typical of all human conflict? If there is any uniqueness, it may be in the depth of the issues. Companies may encounter conflict over decisions about how to treat their staff which are founded in fundamental differences in views about human nature, justice and equality, but in general commercial decisions are on the more pragmatic level of effectiveness, efficiency, quality and value. Political decision-making may also involve choices between very fundamental human value-systems.

But theological issues are founded in our understanding of the nature of God, and of the human nature which reflects the nature of the divine. Thus even apparently trivial matters, such as whether one sits or kneels for prayer, whether one comes forward to receive bread and wine from the altar or is served in one's seat, may be seen as matters of ultimate importance, and thus differences of view can become invested with the weight associated with the defence of ultimate truths. This can 'raise the stakes' in church life at every level, and make the task of the peacemaker more challenging. As the joke has it, 'Are we going to do this in your way, or in God's way?'

The teaching of Jesus Christ implies standards of human behaviour, which may or may not be absolute, but which we are all unable to fulfil all of the time, or indeed, at any time in their totality. Conflict arises within Christian communities when the behaviour of individuals or groups is seen as consistently unacceptable, and as a 'bad witness' to Christ by those who claim to be his disciples. Resolving such conflicts will involve issues about the kind of discipline that is appropriate within the context of Christian love, and of how authority is exercised within communities of faith.

Jesus' own teaching, and that of the early Church preserved in the New Testament, called for the unity, in love, of those who follow him, even though the Early Church showed signs of the opposite from the first! Nevertheless Jesus has given us the ultimate task of reconciliation, between God and humanity, and between human individuals and institutions. However, these are ultimate rather than immediate aims, and a positive approach to conflict will be part of the process by which these ideals are realised.

THE PURPOSE OF THIS BOOK

Our aim in writing this book is to empower those who want to help resolve conflict in the Church, by providing principles, guidelines and tools, both practical and spiritual, for the task, and by pointing people to other resources which they can use. It is founded on the assumption that anyone may be called to be a peacemaker, and that the skills required are fundamental to our humanity, and not specialised in any way, though most of us will need to develop them within ourselves.

It is not a book about particular denominational structures, or about the relative value of different Christian theological positions. We shall be reflecting theologically about the nature of conflict and the means to resolve it, but we do not believe that there is a theology which enables us to avoid conflict altogether.

On the contrary, we are starting from the assumption that the Gospel of Jesus Christ both presupposes and creates conflict. For the teaching and the lifestyle of Jesus was, and is, critical of every human culture, and illuminates the sinfulness of all human systems, as well as every individual. Jesus said that he would turn family members against each other. Christians like to see themselves as 'nice' people, but Jesus 'knew what was in everyone' (John 2:25), and knew that 'it is from within, from the human heart, that evil intentions come' (Mark 7:21).

The reality is that the Gospel of peace and reconciliation sets up conflicts within ourselves, as we become aware of the tension between Jesus' teaching and our own instincts and wishes. Those same tensions are found between individuals, between groups, and between the Church and society as a whole. We have seen the latter in the last couple of decades when the Church of England has produced reports on the nature and causes of urban poverty like *Faith in the City* (Church House Publishing 1985).

RESOLVING CONFLICT: AN END IN ITSELF?

Seeing the process of responding to conflict as a positive one, we are setting out to describe understandings, methods and skills that contribute to conflict resolution, but before we do that we need to ask whether resolving conflict is an end in itself. If conflict is not necessarily a bad thing, is the absence of conflict always good? Surely not: totalitarian regimes can point to the absence of conflict in their populations, though that may indicate only the degree of fear under which people are living, not their agreement with the regime's policies. The family that never argues may be extraordinarily well-adjusted, or it may be unable to cope with disagreement, and this can result in growth and individuality being stunted.

A church without conflict is likely to be a church which is failing to acknowledge the tensions in the society around it, or one which is not addressing the issues of sin and justice and care with which its Lord was concerned. It may have become an escape from 'real life' – a corporate fantasy, or the expression of a disordered need for perfection. A peaceful church, however, is a church where the unity of purpose and the predominance of loving mutual concern are able to overcome the stresses and tensions which are present in any group of people.

Conflicts may be resolved by people with differing views being reconciled, or by compromises being made, or by new and more creative understandings and projects being accepted by everyone. But at other times they will be resolved by groups of people agreeing to separate and pursue their different visions or objectives as Christians. There is little research in this area, but experience shows that churches that have split after a major conflict, sometimes grow more than churches which have resolved their conflicts. So which outcome most advanced the cause of the Gospel? We need to keep an open mind about outcomes as well as about the issues, where Christians are in conflict with each other.

So we start with a number of assumptions:
- that conflict is not a bad thing in itself.
- that it is inevitable in all churches that are living out the teaching
- of Jesus.
- that most conflict is a temporary part of the healthy process by which change and growth comes about.
- that anyone might acquire the qualities needed to help others resolve conflict, but that these take time to develop, and require careful application and reflection.

Peacemaking is something which we learn by doing, and practical courses are more valuable than reading (see Appendix A). So the principles and methods set out in the following chapters will need practising, and there is no insurance against making mistakes. If we cannot tolerate failure, we would do better not to take on the responsibility of helping others resolve conflict.

FOR REFLECTION . . .

Reading   Matthew 10:27-42

Saying of Jesus 'I have not come to bring peace, but a sword.'

(Matthew 10:34)

Reflection   Jesus as the Bringer of Conflict

The life and ministry of Jesus bring conflict. As a child, Jesus is blessed as 'a sign that will be opposed' (Luke 2: 34). The Gospels portray him as being in conflict with all forms of disorder expressed cosmically, in nature, in the area of suffering and death and in the world of spirits. He is basically in conflict with sin, the absence of love. In the setting of his time, he causes controversy through exposing the hypocrisy, the practical unbelief of the religious authorities. Jesus is the prophet, at the end of a long line of prophets, who comes with a new radical call to obedience, whose words divide people into camps. He brings a sword, not peace, to disturb family relationships, all because his radical call to finding life through losing it must have priority (Matthew 10:39).

His very reason for coming is to announce good news for the poor (and not the rich), release of captives (and not support for the powerful), healing for the sick (and not upholding those who do not need a doctor), (Luke 4:16f). Conflict occurs in the temple, in the wilderness, on a lake, in a graveyard, walking with his disciples, in the synagogue, in front of the crowd and before Pilate.

His legacy is reflected in the Early Church, with disputes breaking out between the rigorists and the liberals, the universalists and the particularists (eg Acts 15). The Church as a visible, human organisation follows Jesus in provoking or evoking controversy. One could argue that it was born in conflict and controversy right from the controversial message and action of the Founder and his first disciples, through the controversies of doctrine and practice of the Early Church, to the current Diaspora. The state of our separation did not simply occur by the spreading of the Gospel but also through division and contention. Schism is still with us. Yet we use the term 'Broad Church' to indicate that parties who hold different conflicting views and practices can function together. We have to recognise that, despite the continual call to 'be one', the history of the Church is littered with sectarianism. We have to strive to seek a form of reconciliation where compromise can be reached or where the situation is contained by parties agreeing to disagree.

Conflict can be understood both as something that occurs within the Church and as something that occurs between the Church and some other body outside. There is also that kind of conflict in the Church which arises where its pronounced truths and practices - built on truth, integrity and righteousness - are manifestly contradicted by the darker elements of human nature: greed, selfishness, revenge, and so on, collectively known as sin.

There is no example of Church today so pristine or unblemished that it can point to the absence of conflict. The state of perfect harmony and peace may be something we sing about, but is rare to find (at least this side of the River Jordan).

The Sword of the Spirit

He brings a sword
Not Peace
Not Jesus?
Yes, a sword
Sharp, two-edged
It cuts through apathy
Divides the fat of self-indulgence
From the bone
We pick up the sword
To fight for him

Against the enemy
This is a battle;
We wrestle
Not against flesh and blood
But against
Principalities
Heavenly powers
On the vestry floor
In the Council Room
Or the hypermarket

The sword of the Spirit is sharp
Cutting the ropes that bind us.

Personal exercise

Close your eyes

Picture a sword

Imagine it turning into a dove

Open your eyes when you are ready

Group exercise

Each person to list which five of the following they consider to have priority as Christian behaviour. Discuss the group's findings.

1. gossiping
2. keeping your temper
3. always standing up for yourself
4. working for nothing
5. forgiving an enemy
6. always telling the truth
7. showing righteous anger
8. turning the other cheek
9. forgiving a friend
10. admitting your mistakes

Prayer

Lord, come to us when the storm is at its worst and bring the still peace.

CHAPTER TWO

OUR PERSONAL POSITION

Before we can begin to help others work through situations of conflict, we need to examine ourselves, our motives, our skills and limitations, and the assumptions that we bring to peacemaking, whether they be political, cultural, familial or personal. What we are, and the way we react to situations of conflict may have a considerable effect on the outcome, whether we have a leadership role or not.

Conflicts around us trigger our own inner conflicts, and the kind of responses which we have to our own issues. So we need to understand the conflicts we have within ourselves, and the kind of strategies we employ to deal with them. For instance, a powerful personality in a congregation who is pushing very hard for something, may evoke a very negative response in someone who has found one of their parents particularly powerful and demanding. This response may have nothing to do with the rightness of the cause for which the person concerned is fighting.

More than that; our inner conflicts can become externalised in the community of which we are a part, particularly if we have a leadership role. For instance, the minister who has learned to feel guilty when he is not working will tend to criticise members of his congregation if they propose leisure activities within the church. This may provoke conflict in the church, as some defend the need for relaxation together, and others take the side of the minister by suggesting that the tasks of mission are more worthy of the church's time.

So we cannot help others resolve conflict if we have not first learned to deal with conflict within ourselves. We can begin to do that simply by asking ourselves, whenever we experience conflict around us, what feelings this produces in us, and what situations in our own lives it reminds us of. Talking this through with someone we can trust may help us to understand our own inner world, and relate that to the situation in which we experience conflict. We will be able to respond freely and constructively in conflict situations when we are aware of our own reactions, and feel ourselves to be in control of them. When that is the case, we will be able to use our own reactions as a means of understanding what is happening around us, and so find appropriate and creative responses.

We can learn about our own responses to conflict by testing our responses to questionnaires. One is provided in Appendix B to this book; others can be found in the Mennonite *Mediation and Facilitation Training Manual* (see Appendix A). Are we the sort of person who provokes conflict or appeases people, the sort who backs away from confrontation or accepts it? What kind of function do we tend to fulfil in groups? Knowing our 'natural' responses helps us cope in actual situations of conflict.

PERSONAL STANCE

To have spent time in personal analysis or counselling can be of great value when approaching this kind of work, though it is not a prerequisite, and the leadership of groups in other contexts can also be of great value. Some understanding of the way that groups operate, and the way we operate in them, is essential, (though that experience may be gained in many different ways) and we will come back to this in subsequent chapters.

But the inner integrity which one brings to situations of conflict is the most vital element. That is nowhere better summed up than in Carl R. Rogers' book *On Becoming a Person* (Constable, London 1961). In the section 'Some Significant Learnings' he makes a number of statements which outline a personal position which is as valuable for any kind of mediatorial or facilitation role as it is in the role of counsellor or psychotherapist.

Among those statements are:

- *I find I am more effective when I can listen acceptantly to myself, and can be myself.* To operate as a facilitator in disputes it is valuable not only to understand ourselves, but to be true to ourselves rather than acting something we are not. That does not mean that we will state all that we feel or think, but that we will be aware of it, and act congruently with it.

- *I have found it enriching to open channels whereby others can communicate their feelings, their private perceptual worlds, to me.* This applies to groups as well as to individuals. It is to be ready to enter into what it is like to be part of a group, and to allow people on different sides of a dispute to communicate what this is about for them.

- *I have found it highly rewarding when I can accept another person.* This is equally true of groups of people. Being able to associate with and respect all parties in a conflict helps us facilitate acceptance between them.

- *The more I am open to the realities in me and in the other person, the less do I find myself wishing to rush in to 'fix things'.* Preconceived notions of how conflicts can be resolved, and what is right for any particular community are not helpful to the mediatorial role. We need to approach issues with humility, as someone who wants to learn and, more particularly, with the understanding that it is not us as mediators who will resolve the issue, but the parties concerned. Any solution will be their solution, not ours.

- *Life, at its best, is a flowing, changing process in which nothing is fixed.* What we are involved in with the church is a process which moves people from a 'stuck' position to one where things are more fluid, where change is possible for individuals and for the church as a whole. While our particular role will come to an end at a certain point, the process will be most healthy if it continues beyond the work that we do with the church.

PERSONAL SKILLS: BEING A LISTENER

If we need to listen to ourselves and be aware of what we are feeling when we work with others, we also need to be able to listen accurately to them. This involves a number of things which we may tend to take for granted:

- Listening without prior judgement to what a person is saying so that we hear it as it is meant.

- Being aware of the emotional content of what is being said, and of the way that things are said. Noticing whether the way something is said matches what is being said, or whether there is an incongruity between the meaning of what is said and the tone or feeling of it.

- Noticing when people speak for themselves, and when they speak collectively or anonymously, eg 'We don't do things that way' or 'Some people think that this is a waste of time.'

- Recognising non-verbal behaviour. This will include where people sit; with others, apart, at one side, behind, or outside the group. It will mean being aware of body posture and facial expression, which, like tones of voice, may reflect what is being said, or may contradict it.

If we are listening effectively we will be able to make appropriate responses, among which may be:

- Checking that we have understood by repeating something back.

- Being ready to ask for clarification when we do not feel that we have fully understood something.

- If we notice an incongruity of feeling or posture, to be able to ask a question which explores the feeling, eg 'You say that you think that would be a good solution, but you don't look/sound happy about it. Can you say what you feel about it?'

- If a person speaks collectively or for an anonymous third party to ask them what they themselves feel, eg 'Do you agree with those who think this is a waste of time?' or 'I am not clear who it is who doesn't do things this way? Could you tell us?'

CULTURE AS A FACTOR IN CONFLICT

Churches often reflect the cultural diversity of the communities of which they are a part. If we are to help in the resolution of conflict we need to be aware that cultural differences affect the way people communicate, the values they tend to take for granted, and their perceptions of any process of reconciliation and healing. This means that we need to listen especially carefully for misunderstandings about the way views are expressed and about the meaning of particular words and phrases, and for any stereotyping in people's views of others.

We also need to be aware of the possibility that ethnic, cultural or socio-economic groups will be disempowered within the Church because of the attitudes of others. Some conflicts may seem to be primarily a clash of cultures, and care must be exercised to ensure that cultural differences are respected, and mutual understandings sought. Humility about the limits of our own cultural understandings and a desire to enter into the experience of people in other cultural settings is a vital part of the facilitator's equipment in multi-cultural situations.

THE ETHICAL LIMITS OF MEDIATION

It is important to be aware that there are situations in which a specifically mediatorial role is inappropriate. If we come across, or are involved in, situations where we believe one party is abusing another, or acting to oppress another party, then we cannot act without ensuring that we empower all parties involved to reach a just settlement. While acting equally for both parties in a conflict will be appropriate most of the time, there will be times when we need to acknowledge a more fundamental responsibility to act justly. We should not be able to accept even a mutually agreed settlement which does not recognise the freedom and self-determination of all parties. Rather we must press for change of the structures which perpetuate inequalities and which store up greater conflicts for the future.

For example, if a small group of individuals control the finances of a church, and use that control to prevent a majority of the church from doing what they believe the church should be doing, no settlement that does not deal with the structural injustice should be acceptable to us as mediators. So we will need to be aware of the power issues in what we do, and be clear that we are working to transform unequal power relationships in the direction of equality of power if we are to act responsibly as peacemakers.

FOR REFLECTION ...

Readings   Exodus 2: 11-15: Luke 12:13,14

Saying of Jesus   'Who set me to be a judge or arbitrator over you?'

(Luke 12:14)

Reflection   One greater than Moses

There is the headstrong intervener who rushes in where angels fear to tread. There is the leader who is called in to intervene. Moses is just as much a slave as his fellow

Hebrews, even though he is a leader. He is a mature person; 'grown up'.

His first intervention is disastrous; he destroys the oppressor. Jesus, the leader greater than Moses, is to teach 'love your enemies, do good to them who persecute you'. In his second intervention, when two of his own people are in conflict and have come to blows, Moses has learnt his lesson. He questions the one who has attacked the other as to why he has done it. He is questioned in turn, 'Who made you a ruler and a judge over us?' Moses learned that his fiery intervention solved nothing. He needed wisdom and patience in order to bring harmony, to be the deliverer God wants in the situation of conflict.

Jesus is called in to settle a dispute, a question about the inheritance of two brothers. He is reluctant to intervene. His role is not to lay down new laws and regulations, to settle disputes. He doesn't want to settle the brothers' dispute by giving them the jot and tittle answer or by setting a precedent, just as he makes an ambiguous statement about giving to Caesar what is due to him and to Yahweh what belongs to him. He replies 'Who made me a judge or arbitrator over you?' (Luke 12:14).

Jesus is the leader greater than Moses and greater than Solomon.

> *The Arbiter*
>
> Me – a judge?
> Not me
> I'm more . . . more a background person
> I don't like arguments
> Disputes - not my cup of tea
> Don't ask me
> To pass judgement

Mind you
I wish they didn't happen
These conflicts
There's always some dirt attached –
I'd rather wash my hands of the whole thing

But I suppose
That's what Pilate did.

Personal exercise
'Go-between'
With your eyes closed:
Who comes into your mind when you hear this phrase?
Imagine Jesus on the cross and the thieves either side.
Imagine them joining hands.

Group exercise
The Good Samaritan: Luke 10:29-37
Role play. Choose a person to play one of the characters in the story. Read the story. Reflect. Let each one say what it is like to have been part of the incident and what you feel about the others in the story.

A man
Robbers (2 or more)
A Priest
A Levite
A Samaritan
An innkeeper

Prayer
Lord, give us compassion to help the victims of violence and forgive us for avoiding conflict, for crossing the road when we see trouble.

CHAPTER THREE

PREPARING THE GROUND

Many investment savings accounts today carry an obligatory 'health' warning; 'These accounts can go down in value as well as up.' The same is true of the investment in conflict situations: intervention can make the situation worse. (Look at the chart in Appendix B to see how!)

So before we begin any work with a church that is living with conflict we need to be clear about a number of things. If we already know a lot about the situation we will need to ask ourselves how we feel about the issues. And whether we know much or not, we need to have a clear contract with the church as to the nature and the parameters of our role.

If we are already involved in the situation, as minister, leader or member of the church, then we have to ask ourselves what role we want to take, and then ascertain whether that role is acceptable to the church as a whole. If we already identify with one point of view in a dispute, or are perceived by others as being largely identified with one point of view, then we are going to be ineffective as a mediator. If we care more that one group wins and another loses than that a decision which everybody can live with is agreed, then we can count ourselves out as facilitators. In these circumstances, we can best help by encouraging someone who is perceived to be disinterested to take on the role of peacemaker. This may be someone outside the situation, or it could be someone who is trusted by everyone involved not to take sides.

Practical experience has shown that it is far better not to have one individual taking on the mediatorial role, but to have two. This has a number of advantages; one can lead while the other observes, the person observing can intervene if the one leading is struggling, or comment on the process rather than the issues, and it can also provide the opportunity for less experienced people to learn by working with someone more experienced. But, perhaps most importantly, having two facilitators avoids the most obvious trap in this kind of role: being seen as biased towards one side or another, or in some cases both, by the different factions! Often when the issue over which conflict is happening in a church is addressed by the minister, s/he is seen as siding with one party or another, and as a result the minister may come to be seen as the problem. In the language of group dynamics, the problem is projected on to the minister. Most ministers will have experienced this uncomfortable position at some time or other, if not frequently! Mediators can be similarly targeted if they are working alone. As a pair, they are less vulnerable to accusations of bias.

Where a minister has become the focus of a dispute within a church, s/he needs to be able to step back if s/he is going to be able to help resolve the issue. This will require that s/he states openly that s/he will not try to enforce his/her own personal position on the issue, but will seek to enable the church to arrive at its own decisions and act on whatever decisions are made. This will not be practical where the minister's own conduct or views are at issue. In that case it is vital that a trusted leader within the church, or an outside person, is given the facilitational role. Then the minister can be freed to explain and promote his/her views. There is a danger that if a facilitator is chosen from within the church, that person's personal authority could be enhanced to the point where s/he becomes a threat to the authority of the minister.

Because of these factors, it is important to recognise when a disinterested party from outside the church itself should be called in. Once conflicts have begun to escalate, it can be difficult to reach agreement on anything, including the suggestion that an outside facilitator or facilitators be called in. So it is vital for those who agree to mediate in another community that they secure a clear agreement or contract about their role, even if there are some who are uncertain or unhappy about it.

Some of the factors that should be clarified and agreed before any work is done are:

- Whether the mediator is there to work with the church, its leadership team, its minister, or a combination of those.
- How decisions about the process itself are going to be made.
- Who is chairing the meetings involved.
- The time commitment that everyone is willing to put into this. (An overall limit on the time taken may be agreed, but is generally better left flexible.)
- The frequency of meetings.
- The aims of the process. (This may be in terms of outcome, eg to get agreement on plans for redeveloping the building which can be agreed by everyone, or in terms of the process itself, eg to help the church improve its communication on issues, and find ways of resolving conflicts.)
- Whether the process is a confidential one. Who, if anybody, would be reported to when the process is over, and by whom.
- Whether a report is to be written for the church at the end of the process, and whether that would include a description of the process and/or recommendations to the church.
- Any financial arrangements (expenses, fee).

If at any stage in the process, for this is what any attempt to transform a conflict situation is, either the church or the facilitator sees a need to change the 'contract', it is important that this is discussed, and new terms agreed, otherwise the process itself may be derailed. However, it is important to be aware that an attempt to change the contract may be a strategy by one party to gain some advantage in the whole process, or to sabotage it, and as such would need to be treated as part of the process itself.

FOR REFLECTION ...

Readings   Psalm 33:10; Psalm 107:10-11; Isaiah 11:2,
John 4:7-26

Saying of Jesus   'If you knew the gift of God . . .'
(John 4:10)

Reflection   Wonderful Counsellor

In pastoral settings today, some want to distinguish between advice-giving and counselling. The first can involve both the giving of information and some judgement about a possible way of proceeding for someone in difficulty. Counselling, on the other hand, centres on the client as the centre of decision making. The counsellor explores with the client the various options open and the cognitive and emotive influences in finding a way forward.

Both are person-centred. Some people look for a manual, a know-how course, a set of procedures by which to act, others realise there are no procedures which fit every case but one proceeds 'in faith' using a whole armoury of guides including intuition, hunches, friends' advice and the long-tested 'common sense'.

In the Old Testament, counsel and advice were interchangeable. There was no 'take it or leave it' principle at work, however. To counsel was to express thoughts in words. But these words were always acted upon. When counsel is followed by action, it may be said to 'stand' (Psalm 33:11) or to be 'fulfilled' (Psalm 20:4) (Isaiah 44:26).

The ideal ruler is to be a good counsellor, and a good counsellor is one who has wisdom (Isaiah 11:2). In the New Testament counsel is exercised by God and can mean advice (Hebrews 6:17). Human counselling, both good and bad, is open to God the perfect counsellor, the perfect judge (1 Corinthians 4:4). He knows the counsels of all our hearts. Again, in Romans 11:33-36 'God . . . how unsearchable are his judgements . . . "For who has known the mind of the Lord? Or who has been his counsellor?"' Human discernment is not always accurate. We have to search for truth and speak it in love.

Jesus is the most wonderful counsellor. He knows what is inside us. He perceives, 'looks upon', groans within, asks the right questions, acts consistently and congruently, is not afraid to say what is, (as the Samaritan woman, Nicodemus and the Rich Young Ruler found out).

Truly Awesome

Have you met one? Someone who listens
Knows you and knows where you come from?
Like a good parent
Full of wisdom
A father or mother
Whose influence lasts forever
There's something awesome
About such a person
Wonder-full
They speak peace through their eyes
Prince-like.

Personal exercise

Think of one person who has helped you on your life journey. What was it about that person that made them a good counsellor?

Group exercise

Each member of the group picks one of the following sayings as the one they would think was most generally helpful to someone who is causing friction in the church and obviously doesn't realise it. Discuss your choice together.

1. Repent and believe the Gospel.

2. Could we talk about your action? It's causing me concern.

3. People are talking about you, did you know?

4. Do you realise what effect you are having on others?

5. Can we pray together? I am concerned about something.

Prayer

Lord,
Open our eyes . . . to see your truth
Open our ears . . . to hear your word
Open our hearts . . . to feel your love.

CHAPTER FOUR

TAKING ON A ROLE

In this chapter we will look at the kind of role we take on when we attempt to resolve conflicts in groups. We have used three different terms to describe this role, and each implies a slightly different way of working, though the area of overlap is considerable. *Facilitation* implies that someone is present simply to enable the parties concerned to resolve issues themselves, with the minimum amount of interference, and in a non-directive way. *Mediation* suggests that someone is standing between opposing parties to facilitate communication between them, (not many conflict situations in churches are that simple), and *Peacemaking*, which has a clearer theological basis, and implies a more active role which may be more directive or didactic. It should be said at the outset that there is no one right way of working, and that each person or team will need to find their own preferred method in any given situation.

Whatever approach we take, we bring our own values and principles to the situation, and however little we seek to impress them upon people, they will affect the way that the process goes. So it is important that we understand how we want to operate, and why. So here are some principles and methods you may want to consider.

Firstly, three principles:

1. *You are there for everyone in a conflict.* You are there for the ones holding power and for those without it. You are there for those who are enthusiastic about the process, and for those who see it as a waste of time.

2. *You are not there to determine the outcome, but to enable others to find it.* You are not there to negotiate, but to facilitate others' negotiations. The outcome might be other than you wish, and you might wish to make that point, and

say why, in any report after the event. But the resolution or transformation which occurs has to be the one that the church itself chooses.

3. *Your primary concern is the process itself, not the issues involved.* You are there to create the right environment in which new understandings and resolutions can be found. This will involve making the process a safe one for everyone involved, a place where they can take creative risks without fear of being abused or feeling unsupported. It is vital that you oversee the issues, rather than becoming immersed in them.

In order to help people deal with the issues, recognise the interests involved, and cope with personalities, some techniques are generally helpful:

1. *Explain what you are going to do.* Give people information about what you are proposing to do. If you are going to make suggestions, say that that is what you are about to do. If you are going to seek information, say so. This allows people to prepare themselves, and helps them to feel comfortable.

2. *Test for common understanding.* Check your own understanding of what is being said by repeating back what has been said in your own words. Is that what was meant? Is that what others understood by what was said?

3. *Ask open questions.* Try to avoid questions which have either a yes/no answer, or imply an answer, eg 'What do you see as the good and bad aspects of the plans for the new building?' rather than 'Are you for or against the plans for the new building?'

4. *Summarise.* At regular intervals, and certainly at the end of meetings, summarise what has happened, even if that involves expressing the confusion felt in a meeting. (If confusion exists, it is better that it is acknowledged.) Clarity at every stage helps in decision-making and in restoring bruised relationships.

5. *Allow pauses for reflection, review and replanning.* This can take a number of forms: putting headings on a flip chart or OHP, getting people to reflect in small groups, giving time for silent contemplation or for prayer. It may be important to prevent a new topic or area of concern to be introduced when there will be inadequate time to discuss it, so seek agreement to come back to it at a future session.

6. *Test the reality of statements.* In situations of conflict claims are often exaggerated. When necessary, ascertain whether observable facts bear out the claims being made, eg 'You say that most people here don't want a large candle as a regular feature on the Communion table. Let's find out who does and who does not.'

7. *Emphasise the positive.* Try to respond positively to negative statements, by recognising positive aspects of them, by recognising the helpfulness of having the feeling expressed openly, or by acknowledging that you have understood the feeling.

8. *Encourage people to speak about themselves, not others.* We will come back to this under 'ground rules', but typical attacking behaviour is to speak about the other person rather than oneself. A suitable response to the statement 'Mr A. is trying to get his own way by keeping the facts of the church's financial position from us', might be 'So you believe that Mr A. is not giving the church all the facts. Could you say what has led you to that conclusion?'

9. *Encourage people to describe negative feelings, rather than give vent to them.* 'You seem to be feeling angry, as if you were feeling under attack. Can you say what would help you to feel differently?' Remain cool yourself, but fully engaged with what is being expressed.

10. *Develop options.* Encourage people to consider different options, brainstorm possible alternatives, and ask for suggestions for ways forward.

11. *Explore interests by asking why.* It is helpful to get beyond the positions people take to find out what it is they want, eg 'I understand that you want the minister to leave. Why do you think that will improve the situation as far as you are concerned?'

Although mediation, facilitation and peacemaking are roles, the honesty, openness, care and integrity which you bring to your role will be vital to the spirit in which it is conducted, and to the kind of responses you will get. As in all Christian ministries the qualities of character that we bring to the task are more important than the techniques that we use. However, good intentions are not enough; we need to clear about the principles and the techniques which we are bringing to the role.

(Love your enemies ?)

FOR REFLECTION ...

Reading   Mark 9: 33-35

Saying of Jesus 'The Son of Man came not to be served but to serve . . .'   (Mark 10:45)

Reflection   Towel Service

We live in a society where business is based on doing better than our competitors. The object of it, it is stressed, is to improve our standard of living. Bigger means better. In real terms we are told we need to be better off. We have heard that small is beautiful but that applies more to kittens than bank balances.

Wherever people meet there is always a power struggle; after all power (authority, influence) is a force. We carry with us the forces which we have either appropriated ourselves or had bestowed upon us by others. There is the power which comes through innate charisma. Jesus was certainly a charismatic authority who told Pilate that all authority on earth and in heaven had been given to him.

Yet he 'emptied himself of all but love and bled for Adam's helpless race'. He did not snatch at being equal with the greatest authority of all but took the form of a servant and made himself of no reputation and humbled himself, dying on a cross (Philippians 2:5-8). We call this *kenosis*, self-emptying.

This is the hardest thing to show in the Church. Every organisation tends to develop a hierarchy, to have someone in charge 'above them'. The Church is no exception. But when the Teacher himself takes a towel and washes the learners' feet, that is something different. When the Leader shares power with the led, that is something different.

The world is beginning to learn it. It calls it 'empowerment'. It doesn't mean taking power and control to oneself, it means enabling the power in the other to be set free and exercised. Where is the power in your church, and what model of leadership does your church practice ?

Priorities

There comes a time
A moment when we're back in the house
At home,
That someone asks
What was happening back there
What was the argument all about?

31

On the road we like a conversation
Sometimes we want to assert ourselves
Know where we are in the pecking order

He had heard them behind him on the road
Arguing . . .
But now they were quiet
Silent, noncommittal
No need to say anything
He knew,
There was no hiding anything from him

He sat down
Gathering the twelve around him
In the living room, perhaps?
Who's first, who's last?
Let me tell you
You want to be top dog?
Learn to be underdog
To get a first
You have to be last.

Personal exercise
Ask yourself honestly
Is there anything you would feel so strongly about that you
would leave the church if the majority thought differently
from you?

Group exercise
Try to share the above conclusions each of you came to.

Prayer
Lord, guide our conversation as we go
and help us to find our true status as we walk.

CHAPTER FIVE

WORKING WITH THE CHURCH

1: Starting the process

While every church situation is different, and every process of peacemaking unique, there are some general patterns which emerge in effective processes of reconciliation. An awareness of these, as a guide rather than a strait-jacket, can help in the preparation for meetings, and provide a general sense of direction for the process.

CREATING A SAFE ENVIRONMENT

Creating a safe environment in which people can open up is vital at the beginning of the whole process. This involves establishing trust and confidence, and there are a number of ways in which you can do this:

- Introduce yourself, giving your understanding of why you are there, and explain that you see your task as facilitating a process, not determining its outcome. You will suggest ways of proceeding, but the agenda, and the outcome, is for those in the meeting to determine.

- Suggest that each meeting begins and ends with worship, so that the whole process is grounded in the group's common faith in the Christ who has called all of them to a ministry of reconciliation.

- Offer some ground rules for the meetings, which you will help people to observe, and seeking agreement to them:
    1. The meeting will finish by . . . (one and a half hours is probably long enough). The meeting will only be extended by explicit agreement with everybody.
    2. Speak only for yourself, and if you must speak for someone else, identify that person.
    3. Do not speak in the first person plural; in other words, on behalf of groups, whether you identify them or not.

4. Speak about issues, not personalities.

5. Do not speculate on, or make assumptions about, the motives of others.

6. Listen with respect, and in silence, to others, so that people are not interrupted. (You may want to reassure people that you will ask anyone who takes too much of the meeting's time to give others a chance to speak.)

- If you are discussing issues of confidentiality, should what is said at this meeting go no further, or should others, like church members who cannot be present, or other family members, be put in the picture? This is especially important with leadership groups like elders, deacons, church councils or PCCs. It is advisable to get specific agreement from each person in such groups; it is surprising how often individuals allow themselves to think that generally agreed rules of confidentiality do not apply to them! You should point out that there are some things that cannot, by law, be kept confidential, including child abuse and serious crime; if these come to light, they must be reported to the appropriate authorities.

- Check with the meeting that they share your understanding of the aims of the process in which you are all involved. If not, make sure that they are redefined, and written down in some form, so that they can be referred back to later.

GATHERING INFORMATION

Once the ground rules are agreed the first priority is likely to be one that can be seen in two ways: as allowing everyone present to say what they want to say about the situation, and as the gathering of information by the mediator/s. It may be helpful to have a brainstorming session at the outset, asking people to name all the aspects of the present situation which are causing discomfort, whether they be big or small, and simply writing them on a flip chart. They can then be prioritised or grouped later, and referred back to when it comes to checking that everything has been covered.

Some suggestions to facilitate this part of the process are:

- Encourage every person to speak if they have things they want said. Remind people that though it may be difficult to speak in a meeting, it is their responsibility to say what they want said, rather than feeling frustrated, or complaining after the meeting that something was not said!

- Encourage people to say what they would like to get out of this process, not only what they think is wrong at the moment.

- Offer each person the opportunity to speak only once during this first period, but allow the whole of the first session for this activity if it is needed.

- Point out that this is not a debate, and encourage people to say what they want to say without reference to what others have said.

- Try to prevent discussion at the outset from becoming focused too narrowly on one issue; point out that you want to get the whole picture first, and that there will be time to discuss every issue once the whole picture has emerged.

- Where there is a straightforward division over one central issue it may be helpful to ask people what they see as the likely results of failing to find agreement about a way forward. (What is known in negotiating terminology as BATNAs; Best Alternatives To No Agreement.)

- When everyone who wants to has spoken, reflect back to the meeting what you have heard and observed, eg the numbers present, the absence of individuals or groups, the principle issues, the kind of feelings being expressed, the numbers speaking for particular points of view, and the number of those who have been silent. Ask whether your impressions have been accurate, but limit the time for responses at this stage.

- Ask questions to confirm things which you think have been implied, but not actually stated, eg 'Do you think that the principle problem here is not the minister, but the disagreements within the church about the kind of changes s/he has been proposing?' 'Have some people found it difficult to accept decisions made by the church meeting?'

- Ask about, or confirm, the objectives of the whole process. This may have to be revised from the purpose initially suggested as a result of what has been heard, eg 'We were asked to come and help you resolve your differences with your minister, but it sounds as if there are major disagreements within the church. Do you want to make it your aim to resolve these, as well as improving the relationship with your minister?'

Make sure that people are gently but firmly reminded of the ground rules they have agreed to if they start to break them. If necessary suggest how remarks could be rephrased, or check on matters of fact, eg 'Do you mean that you feel angry because you suspect that it is the minister who wanted to move the choir to the side of the church? Perhaps we could check the facts at some point with members of the group who made the decision.'

If these opening activities take the whole of the first session, as they usually do, make sure of the following:

- that you give warning ten minutes or a quarter of an hour before the finishing time that time is limited.
- that you leave time for at least a moment of quiet reflection and prayer before people depart.
- that you obtain agreement to continue the process (or otherwise!), and on the date of the next meeting.

RECORDING MEETINGS

It is important to keep notes of meetings, recorded as soon as possible after the events, so that the process to date can be brought to mind before subsequent meetings. It can often be valuable to be able to quote what people have said, or share impressions or feelings that you have experienced in previous sessions. It is vital that such notes remain confidential from anybody except a co-worker, during and after the process.

While it is important officially to record decisions made during meetings, agreements reached, or the names of people who have agreed to take on particular tasks, it is in general far better that records of interchanges and disagreements are not put into writing for public consumption. It may be advisable to discourage people from putting things in writing to each other while the tensions and disagreements within a church are being discussed. This is because strong feelings committed to print often give more offence than those spoken in a face-to-face situation, and may be a source of embarrassment later.

I bought him to help with parish work!

FOR REFLECTION . . .

Reading   The Book of Jonah

Saying of Jesus   'One greater than Jonah is here!'
                                        (Matthew 12:41)

Reflection   Market Prophets

In today's world none of us is too far from a city. The process of urbanisation is throwing us together. What has the Church to do with the city? Each of us is a missionary called to go into it. Some find God calling them to the countryside, where they believe he is, his handiwork seen clearly in the natural world, the hills, the flowers, the animals, works of his creation.

But Jonah went into the city. That's what God wanted him to do His message was certainly to the point and, like all who bring a message of liberation, like John and Jesus after him, the message is to repent. Change your heart, mind and ways, or else!

The Church needs to do its market research to find how best it can put its message over. People don't listen. Perhaps we are using a language they don't understand. Perhaps they no longer fear punishment or expect the wrath of God to fall upon them. The prophets of doom and gloom never do the market any good.

The Church should be disappointed about this. Sometimes we are at odds with each other about our calling, our methods, our message, even about who is really sending us and the clarity of the message we carry. Sometimes evangelists are successful, sometimes not. We can get disheartened about poor effectiveness, like Jonah. We can certainly feel at odds with the Church that sends us. Even when we are successful, the temptation is to think we haven't done well enough. Guilt always plays its part. We can get very angry as well. Angry with everything, including God. But Jesus wept over the city and more than that, he died close by.

Castor Oil

Angry? Very angry?
There's always someone
Something close at hand
To shelter you from your own passion

Giving you shade when the heat is on
When you sit seething
Red in the face
(Or some other strong colour)

And when the shelter collapses –
Only a passing shield
Against the rage within
Leaving you exposed again –
Remember this, you have seen the palms of Christ
Wounded for you.

Personal exercise
Close your eyes, clench your fists, frown, grit your teeth. Say to yourself 'I'm angry about . . .' Be aware of the word you finish with.
Open your eyes and relax your body and say to yourself 'Peace'.

Group exercise
Each member of the group shares as honestly as possible one thing that makes them angry about the Church and one thing that makes them happy.

Prayer
Lord, help us to use our anger in the cause of righteousness and may nightfall find us at peace.

CHAPTER SIX

WORKING WITH THE CHURCH

2: Developing the process

AGREEING A PLAN OF ACTION

Once everybody has had a chance to speak, and there is agreement that all the issues, as far as people are aware, are now openly on the table, you may want to propose a plan of action which will enable the issues to be confronted, and agreements, conclusions or transformations to be arrived at.

For example, if a number of issues have been presented, a plan of action may involve simply suggesting that the issues are prioritised, and the most important ones addressed first. It may also be helpful to give some indication of a time-scale for the process. This could be to suggest the need for at least one more meeting, or to suggest that a number of meetings are likely to be necessary, and that this could take months rather than weeks! Whatever plans are suggested or made, it is important to keep them open-ended, with a recognition that there may need to be changes in view of new information or developments. (An example of a plan for working with a leadership team can be found in Appendix C.)

WORKING WITH ISSUES AND RELATIONSHIPS

There are two main aspects of the process of conflict transformation which you need to keep in mind throughout. The first concerns the issues at stake, and the means by which issues can be resolved. The second concerns the relationships between people and groups within the church, or within the leadership of it. The exposition of the issues should give indications of some of the relationship problems, whether or not these are openly acknowleged, and how large a factor these are in the conflict as a whole.

For example, a PCC presented itself as having a problem with its vicar. He was accused of riding roughshod over people's wishes. He in turn complained of a lack of pastoral care and personal support being offered to him. At the initial meeting with the group a large number of issues were raised about which there was tension; so many indeed, that it seemed unlikely that they were the problems in themselves; rather it seemed that the PCC was having difficulties in functioning adequately. In that situation the outside consultants felt that it was the relationships and the teamworking that needed work, rather than the original issues. (It turned out that the vicar was not the main problem, and was instead very much part of the solution.)

So in order to achieve a satisfactory transformation of the situation, both issues and relationships needed to be addressed. We will look at some means of addressing each in turn.

WORKING WITH ISSUES

- Work at issues one at a time; you can start with a small issue if the tension is high, but generally it is better to deal with the biggest issue first. (People tend to gravitate towards it.)
- Encourage people to bring out all aspects of the issue. If you know, or suspect, that things are being held back, or people are afraid to speak, ask questions, and encourage people who are silent to participate.
- Try to discover the root causes, including historical ones – some conflicts go on for generations within churches, and affect one minister after another.
- Pick up suggestions and compromises made by people in the meeting, or offer your own. Find out what others think about them.
- Notice strong feelings, and comment upon them, so that they are in the open, eg 'You clearly feel very strongly

about this; could you tell us what you feel, and why this issue affects you in this way?'

- If the whole group is getting stuck, suggest other ways of working:
    1. In small groups: let groups of four try to reach a solution, then join them together to form groups of eight, and ask them to find a solution, then bring those back to the whole meeting. Or ask individuals to write their own solutions before getting into small groups.
    2. In a 'goldfish bowl': ask three or four people to form a circle inside the larger circle of the meeting, to discuss the issues. Only those in the bowl can speak. Anyone in the larger group wanting to speak must tap one of those in the bowl on the shoulder, and wait to be allowed to take their place.
    3. Pros and cons: divide a flipchart sheet into two vertically, and write the advantages of particular suggestions and their consonance with the Gospel on one side and the disadvantages and variance with the Gospel on the other.
- Emphasise areas of agreement, common interests and goals. Make sure that they are recorded.
- Be prepared to meet with interest groups or leadership groups if necessary.
- When a majority has agreed on something, check out how those in the minority feel, and whether they can live with the decision of the majority. Record any decisions, including any details that are necessary for the implementation of the decision. (Like when, where, how, and who by.)
- Examine the decision-making process in the church by discovering how a contentious decision came to be made and implemented (or not implemented!). Whose idea was it? Where was it discussed? Who made decisions about it? How was it implemented? How was opposition to it expressed? This may tell you much about

how the structures in the church work, and how they are used by individuals and groups to achieve their aims. Notice who gets disempowered in the process.

WORKING WITH RELATIONSHIPS

- Model the concern to understand other people's points of view, respect for them as people, and the acceptance and control of strong feelings. Your behaviour will greatly influence the behaviour of others.
- Do not be afraid to confront people about issues or about their behaviour, but be sure before you do that you can do it calmly and with respect.
- Be prepared to arrange meetings with individuals or interest groups where there is a difficulty about addressing their needs and situation within the larger meeting. Obtain the agreement of everyone to these arrangements.
- Notice negative dynamics within meetings, for instance:
  1. *Personalising issues.* 'It is always Jo who tries to stop progress in this church.' Say that you notice that Jo is being identified with a concern about change, and ask if there are not others who share Jo's concern.
  2. *Polarisation.* When a complex set of interests and wishes get simplified into which side people are on, and people's actual feelings and views are dismissed as being 'what they think'. Ensure that issues are dealt with separately, and that people are listened to with care and respect.
  3. *Scapegoating.* When one person is singled out as the cause of all the problems, and everyone accepts that, rather than face the issues. It is often the minister who is scapegoated! It may be helpful to ask whether, if the minister left, people felt that the problems would cease to exist.
  4. *Triangling.* 'Don't you think that Mary should apologise for her behaviour?' You are being drawn into a personal dispute. Acknowledge the feeling

behind the question, but put it back where it belongs, with the person who expressed it. 'So you think that Mary should apologise for her behaviour. Could you say why? Then we will ask Mary how she feels about that'.

5. *Sabotage*. This can take a number of forms:

   - Non-attendance at meetings: significant absences need to be acknowledged and discussed, without judgements being made about the absent person's motives

   - Walking out of the meeting, or being silent in an intimidating or provocative way: such behaviour needs to be challenged in as gentle a way as possible. 'I must admit that I am feeling uncomfortable about your silence. Could you tell us what you are thinking or feeling at the moment?

   - Challenging the role of the facilitator, or denying any value in the proces accept the feeling or opinion being offered, but refer back to the meeting as to check the view of the majority.

   - Trying to force a premature ending to the proceedings, by forcing a vote, or some other means: ask whether others feel that they are ready to come to a conclusion.

- Be prepared to offer exercises or games to help team-building, establish trust, or express feelings. Church groups may be unprepared for this approach, but many individuals will have had experience of this in their work settings. Such exercises are easier to organise and make effective in leadership groups than in whole church meetings, but there can be a place for them there. See Appendix (i) for some examples of exercises, and where to find suitable ones for your particular needs.

Working with issues and relationships will often bring up difficulties with the structures within the church. Changes to church structures may be a necessary part of the decision-making within the process, or they could form the subject of a recommendation to the church at the end of the process.

'Why am I my brothers' Keeper?'

FOR REFLECTION ...

Reading   Matthew 5:1-11

Saying of Jesus 'Blessed are the peacemakers.'
                     (Matthew 5:11)

Reflection   The Go-Between

Peacemakers are not born. They have to develop certain characteristics. They need courage, tenacity, negotiating skills, the ability to listen to all sides, to arbitrate. Occasionally they will be shot at in the crossfire even though they are waving the white flag.

In the early days of Christianity there was only sporadic peace for the new Christians. The Romans saw them as troublemakers, atheists who wouldn't pledge allegiance to the Emperor; superstitious because they believed in a strange god who they celebrated by drinking wine and eating bread. Christians were tortured, imprisoned, thrown to lions, burnt at the stake in those first centuries of growth. The blood of the martyrs was the seed of the Church.

The one who stands between people to try and make peace is a mediator. He or she is also in danger of being a scapegoat. The community that sent a goat into the desert carrying their sins believed that this reconciled them, both to each other and to God.

There are scapegoats in our own society, those who bear the punishments and insults that should be directed elsewhere. They bear the marks of their ordeals. There is an obvious relationship between vicar and vicarious. The peacemaker sometimes acts as a substitute for the intended victim.

The cross of Jesus is a place that makes peace. It is the place where life and death contend. It is the place where the burden of responsibility from above meets the horizontal of the everyday human. This is the place where Jesus the Lamb of God bears the weight and 'by his stripes we are healed'.

Children of God

They wave white flags
The children of God
They stand in the firing line
The children of God
They offer cheeks to be hit
Walk a second mile with the soldier
Forgiving those who owe them money
Their only goal
To reconcile enemies
Change hate for love
The children of God
Are always in danger
Of spilling blood.

Personal exercise
Close your eyes.
Hold up both hands.
Imagine your best friend in your right hand and your worst enemy in your left hand.
Bring your hands slowly together.
Open your eyes.

Group exercise
Pass the peace round the group by shaking hands or other suitable gesture and saying, 'The Peace of Christ be with you.' Discuss what a peaceful church would be like.

Prayer
Lord, make us instruments of your peace; where there is hatred let us bring your love; where there is injury, your pardon; where there is doubt, true faith; where there is despair, hope; where there is darkness, light; where there is sadness, joy. (St Francis of Assisi)

CHAPTER SEVEN

WORKING WITH THE CHURCH

3: Objectives, outcomes and conclusions

As in the previous stages of a healing or conflict resolution process, it is important for the facilitator to oversee the planning of endings, and to seek agreement at every stage. Clarity and agreement about endings can make a considerable difference to the outcomes beyond the process, and though these cannot always be tidy and comfortable, every effort should be made to finish in a positive, forward-looking manner.

It should be pointed out that while there is an ending to the process with the facilitator or mediator in a healthy process, the process itself will not end when the facilitator leaves, but will continue in the life of the church in various ways. It is not uncommon for churches or leaders' groups to realise months or years later that outcomes of the process are still being realised. Ongoing creative tensions may be of more value than an absence of all conflict.

Different styles of intervention imply different outcomes, and these will be seen in the ongoing activity and implementation that result from the peacemaking, facilitation or mediation.

REVIEWING THE ORIGINAL AIMS OF THE PROCESS

- Review how far the original aims of the process have been achieved.
- Ask what remains to be done.
- Check that implementations have been agreed in detail.

This may be all that is necessary by way of concluding the process.

SETTING NEW OBJECTIVES FOR THE CHURCH

If the conflicts have been more about relationships than issues, or a lack of vision and shared understanding of the purpose of being church has come to light, it may be helpful to encourage the church to conclude the process of reconciliation by agreeing a new mission statement for the church. This will help to strengthen the sense of unity within the church, and also help it to move on from unhealthy forms of conflict to achieve new aims.

The new aims and objectives can be brainstormed and negotiated, or small groups can bring suggestions to the wider meeting. The process of forming a new church mission statement can provide a teaching tool for the church, enabling it to start afresh by making decisions and implementing them in healthy ways. But above all it helps to orientate the church towards its future, and towards hope, based on its Christ-centred and Spirit-empowered task.

ENDINGS

- As with individual meetings, it is important to signal the end of the process before it arrives, so that any unfinished business can be identified and dealt with.
- Review, with the church, what has happened, from your perspective, and sum up what you believe has been achieved. Invite others to say what they see as having been of value in the process.
- Finish, if it seems appropriate to everybody, with a special act of worship, celebrating what has been achieved, and committing the future of the church into God's service and God's keeping.
- Make it clear, if necessary, that there will be no further involvement as facilitator unless there is a fresh approach from the church, and a fresh contract agreed.
- As with individual meetings, review what has happened with your co-facilitator, if you have one, after the event. Write down the broad outlines of what has happened, and the details of what has been decided.

- If you have agreed to do so, write a report for the church. This may include a description of the process, and of the church itself, and recommendations for further action or reflection. Keep it confidential unless the church has specifically agreed otherwise.

I'm sorry we are a closed order!

FOR REFLECTION ...

Reading   Matthew 28:16-20

Saying of Jesus 'All authority in heaven and on earth has been given to me'.

(Matthew 28:18)

Reflection   Power Dressing

Power and influence are what a lot of people are looking for. Traditionally, I suspect, power has largely been attributed to men and influence more to women! There are a number of ways of gaining power and, once gained, of holding on to it. Once we have been granted power and authority and status in the Church, we are reluctant to give it up easily. Those who hold high office in the Church must find it hard to work again 'in the lower ranks'. We all know of people who have kept their positions for years. Loss of status can be a loss of identity, what the existentialists call 'non-being'. It can be devastating for people.

The powers that be, at any one time, are subject to popular will unless they are seen to have a divine right. Influence, however, is less identifiable. It is not necessarily supported by instruments which uphold power – the power of force and the ballot-box, for example.

We are under influence when we let something flow into us, whether it is the words of an advertising slogan, the presence of a charismatic figure or the food or drink we consume.

Pilate thought he had the power to release Jesus or crucify him. What Pilate didn't acknowledge was that not just his power and authority but all authority was 'given from above'. He knew that his power was given to him through the emperor's seal. His oath of allegiance to the emperor was a recognition that divinity lay with the Lord Caesar himself. Any crown he wore was given to him from above in Rome. Most societies are controlled by a domination system of some sort. The hierarch, the master, though subject to the democratic process where it exists, has been given authority to take control.

But the power of Jesus is seen in his powerlessness. He is stripped of his clothes and given a mock crown of thorns and a mock kingly robe. He allows himself to be humiliated and spat upon and gambled over. His power and influence lie in the example of love which lays aside splendour and bleeds. Paradoxically the final humiliation, the crucifixion itself, has the greatest influence. 'And I, when I am lifted up from the earth, will draw all people to myself' (John 12:32). According to Matthew, the power and authority of Jesus was transmitted to the disciples in order that they should to go out and make disciples of all nations. The power in the

Church is not to be for the few but for all to find their way to baptism into the Church.

Fugue

There are times when we run
From power in all its forms
One thing after the other
Demanding our attention
We long to follow another tune
More exciting and stronger perhaps
Calling us to cope better

Here we are promised eternal sounds
Beyond the ordinary
Counterpoints to our dull lives
Shaking monotony

It's as if we don't live in this land
Though we are here singing hymns
Smiling at each other every Sunday
Collecting up the books
Counting the money afterwards
As the organist continues
Lost in his own world.

Personal exercise
Reflect for a minute or two. Do you feel 'called' to something? What prevents you from responding?

Group exercise
All except one hold hands. Appoint a person to squeeze a hand to the left or right of them. The 'outsider' has to guess where the 'power' has got to. What happens to the power in your church? Where does it stop?

Prayer
Lord of all power and truth and grace, let us feel your power in our veins, know your truth in our hearts and share your grace in our eyes.

CHAPTER EIGHT

DEALING WITH DISAGREEMENTS BETWEEN MINISTER AND CHURCH

So far the role or the involvement of the minister or ministers of a church in the process of conflict resolution has not been discussed. It is obviously vital to be clear about ministers' involvement in situations where they are the focus of the conflict, but it is also important to examine the way that they are involved in any such process.

1. The minister should have access to separate and confidential support through the process. This should be provided by someone other than the facilitator/s of the process. If they are a part of a team providing peacemaking, no information will be passed from the minister's support-person unless specific permission has been given for that to happen.

2. Even in situations where the minister is under attack from the church the minister should not be excluded from the process, unless s/he refuses to take part.

3. Where the minister and church are in conflict there remains, throughout the process, the possibility that the minister will decide to resign, that the church may ask her/him to leave, or that the minister's level of stress will result in sick leave being necessary. In any of these circumstances continued support will be vital.

4. It is important to recognise from the start that one resolution of conflict between a minister and a church is that they part company, and that this may be the right, or the best obtainable, solution. However, as with marriage, the assumption should be made that the relationship is valuable, and should be preserved until there is agreement by both parties that it is beyond repair.

If the minister is to be involved in the task of transforming conflict, there are two ways that this can happen: firstly, that the minister shares in the leadership of the process, or secondly, that s/he is treated as any other member of the church for part, or all, of the process.

The involvement of the minister in the leadership of the process looks attractive, because it appears to shore up her/his authority, and confirm her/his position of leadership. However, making the minister part of the leadership of the process makes it far more difficult for her/him to recognise her/his place in the community, and the effect that that position has on others. The minister is part of the dynamics of the situation, and if there is to be healing and renewal, the minister as a person contributing to the situation, must be part of that process.

Freed from the responsibility of controlling events for the period of the facilitators' involvement, the minister has the opportunity to gain a new perspective on their role and involvement, and the feeling that that engenders in them and in others. It may also allow others in the church to see the minister in a new light, and particularly as a person apart from the particular role s/he has as minister, and leader of the fellowship.

The loss of power involved in their handing over the leadership of the process to an outside facilitator is one which would need careful handling by the person providing individual support. Their role would be to encourage the minister to see this time as an opportunity for learning about themselves and about their interaction with the church as a whole, and for getting feedback from others about how, as persons as well as ministers, they are perceived.

By being encouraged to reflect themselves on the process taking place within the church, they can be helped to find new ways of exercising leadership which might be more effective for the church and for themselves. This might well involve allowing and encouraging leadership within the church to be more shared.

If the minister is to be present on the same basis as everyone else, this needs open acknowledgement at the very beginning of the process, with reasons perhaps being given, so that the church as well as the minister is encouraged to see this in a positive light.

In situations where the minister is the focus of discontent, the first stage of the process will obviously be a painful one, and s/he will have the same opportunity to speak, and limitations on speaking, as others. Feedback from the facilitator/s may include some reflection on the position that the minister appears to be in.

The second stage of the process will provide the opportunity for the minister to own their particular personal position about issues, and perhaps explain how that impacts upon their role in leadership. It may also be useful to reflect on the minister's position in relation to groups within the church; whether they feel accepted, whether leadership is required from her/him in them, or whether they feel excluded from particular groups.

In the third stage the minister may want to be an active participant in the setting of aims and objectives, or more of an observer. It may be important to identify publicly whether s/he feels included or excluded from any or all of them, and from the process for achieving them described by the meeting.

It would be helpful if the minister is asked to provide closing worship at the final meeting, so that her/his role is re-established and affirmed.

If, as a result of the process, the minister declares an intention to leave, or actually removes her/himself from the process in advance of leaving, the facilitators will need to allow room for people to express their feelings about that. It will, of course, alter the agenda for the process as a whole, and that will need to be revised. With this, as with other worst-case scenarios, facilitators would do well to consider how they would respond to such an event before it happens.

FOR REFLECTION ...

Reading   John 14: 25-31

Saying of Jesus 'Peace I leave with you; my peace I give to you'.

                                         (John 14:27)

Reflection   Moving On

When someone we cherish and value leaves a church we can feel let down. If we have invested a lot – our emotional interest , our money, our time – in one particular person, a leader or a minister, their departure leaves us at a loss. Ministers come and go, however. Each leader has their own gifts and experiences to offer to the congregation and community. Most effective, however, is the minister who can draw out the abilities, gifts and experiences of the congregation.

In some traditions, of course, the idea of a paid clergy person or minister is irrelevant. Congregations find their own form of organisation and leadership. Nevertheless when a key figure leaves for one reason or another, then there is a loss, a form of bereavement.

When Jesus was about to leave his disciples, their hearts were troubled, they were afraid. But he promised not to leave them comfortless. He would leave his peace – his Shalom – with them. This would be brought about through the Holy Spirit. The opposite to Shalom is chaos, disharmony, contention, alienation, enmity. But where Jesus is present there is Shalom. We are not left in the dark as to how we can achieve Shalom. The Holy Spirit, says Jesus, will 'teach' us all things.

We may sometimes think that God is absent. Paradoxically, however, the absent Father is the God who is with us. He may be hidden from our sight but we need not be worried or afraid. If only we had this assurance, this confidence, this trust that all will be well, despite the absence of the things that visibly reassure us. Ultimately we are not dependent on any external person. Those who preach in the pulpit or visit us in our difficulties or administer the sacraments to us may inspire us, support us, or challenge us. But if our lives are dependent on them for our continuing well-being, then we will be vulnerable.

Coming or going, staying or leaving, being present or being absent, our faith is based on the Christ who lives amongst us. Where we gather together, whoever we are, he is there with us. As Bonhoeffer said, 'Christ exists as community.' Coming and going are part of the cycle of existence, and the Christian community learns when it perceives change as opportunity rather than threat.

The Real Jesus

We are always looking for the real
And not the fake,
The drink, the sport, the language
The pseudo will never be good enough
There is no such thing
As the genuine imitation
Jesus is really there
When we meet
In the breaking of bread
In the word illumined
In the stranger befriended
The prisoner visited

Significant people do come and go
What remains is us
Together, a community of saints
Some here, some departed
Virtual reality is not enough
Jesus said, 'I am with you always.'

Personal exercise
Spend a minute or two reflecting on what would you most
miss about your church.

Group exercise
Each person to share their thoughts with the group. What
does this say about the church community?

Prayer
Lord, help us to believe when we do not see and to see even if
we do not believe.

CHAPTER NINE

DEALING WITH INDIVIDUAL DISPUTES OVER DISCIPLINARY ISSUES

What happens when people in a church are considered by some to have behaved in a way inconsistent with the Gospel and the accepted standards of the Church? And how far should any response from a church be affected by the individuals concerned being casual adherents, church members, church officers, elders, voluntary workers like youth and children's leaders, or paid employees like caretakers, organists or directors of music?

We may like to believe that serious incidents or problems are few and far between in church life. Sadly this is not so; the Christian Church is as likely as other organisations to encounter major dilemmas about the behaviour of its members. Often these arise quite unexpectedly and strike the church like a bombshell. Some examples are:

- prominent members of the congregation leaving their marital partners to live together.
- the discovery of financial irregularities.
- allegations of child abuse within the congregation.
- church employees like caretakers accused of failing to do their job adequately.
- people's sexual practices privately or publicly revealed.
- serious conflicts over matters of principle or practice.

At such times the peace and unity of the congregation can be seriously threatened, and church leaders are often uncertain about how to proceed. The pressures created by strong feelings and confusion add to the difficulties. At such moments an outside facilitator may be helpful.

PRINCIPLES OF DISCIPLINE AND PASTORAL CARE

It is perhaps more consistent with the Gospel of Christ to ask how the church may become more tolerant of difference, and inclusive in its behaviour, than to use discipline as a starting-point in considering the behaviour of church members and adherents.

We are reminded that our Lord came not to judge, but to save the world (John 12:47). In the one passage in the Gospels dealing with discipline among Jesus' followers, as well as suggesting how to approach the erring brother or sister, Jesus emphasises the importance of repeated forgiveness (Matthew 18:15-35).

We are called by the apostle Paul to a recognition and acceptance of the difference of others (1 Corinthians 12:12-27) and a concern for a wholeness that is inclusive. Romans 15:1-7 also speaks about mutuality rather than the exclusion that Paul nevertheless does countenance in the extreme situation (1 Corinthians 5). We are called to a ministry of reconciliation with each other and with God (2 Corinthians 5:18-19) and that takes priority over our natural desire to exclude those who do not conform to our own patterns of behaviour.

We often describe the Church as a family, and it is an apposite metaphor. The family can be the primary support unit that nourishes its individual members, but the family can also be dysfunctional. The reality is that the family frequently acts as the disciplining unit that controls. The child hears a parental message that says 'should' and 'don't' and is restrained from exploring different ways. The underlying message that is received by the child is 'There is something wrong with you. It is not OK to be you, it is only OK to be what we want you to be.'

Churches can also act as the 'bad parent', telling the child what to do without concern for the child's own individuality:

'Do as I do.'

'Do not do anything that embarrasses me or makes me feel uncomfortable.'

'Do not behave in a way that may draw attention to me.'

Churches tend to enforce, control, discipline and exclude, instead of allowing people to treat each other as responsible adults.

As we face issues of the behaviour of others we are faced with our own 'shadow' – the dark side of each of us. In our dealings with people we can learn to make a relationship with the shadow part of ourselves, rather than uing others as scapegoats. 'Darkness and light are the same to you' (Psalm 139). In the language of Jesus, we should see the beam in our own eyes before assessing the speck in another's (Matthew 7:3). (See Steve Shaw: *Dancing with your Shadow*, Triangle, SPCK 1995.)

DISCERNING DIFFERENT KINDS OF BEHAVIOURAL ISSUES

Having looked at general principles of understanding and care, we need to distinguish between different kinds of behaviour, in order to decide what kind of responsive action is appropriate. If in any, and all, situations, ministers and churches are in any doubt about their capacity to deal with an issue, they should seek help from appropriate sources. Denominational organisations will be able to provide information on whom to consult.

CRIMINAL BEHAVIOUR

At the most serious level there is behaviour which demands that you act immediately to prevent harm to individuals. The foremost example is child abuse.

In the case of child abuse you should ensure that the church responds in the ways indicated in denominational guidelines, complying with The Children Act of 1989. The appropriate authorities for dealing with the matter should be identified and contacted directly. If the church has not yet adopted these guidelines, then local Social Services should be contacted to tell you who should be informed. If you are in any doubt as to whether the seriousness of the matter merits professional involvement, check with the professionals themselves – do not rely on your own judgement. If you fail to act on information you receive, you could be liable to charges yourself. Do not try to resolve instances of child abuse by internal means; experience shows that you are likely to make matters worse.

Confidentiality should be preserved in this matter as far as possible, for the sake of the child or children concerned. However, this cannot mean protecting from the proper authorities the identity of people against whom accusations of abuse have been made. Where possible, anyone who confesses abuse should be encouraged to seek qualified medical help.

The healing of the church community where such abuse becomes public knowledge may well be very difficult and painful for those in leadership as well as those involved more directly, but a determination to avoid the issues if possible will not aid such healing, but may make those who are hurt feel discounted and further abused. (See Patrick Parkinson, *Child Sexual Abuse and the Churches*, Hodder & Stoughton.)

Other forms of behaviour which could result in criminal proceedings and which become public knowledge should, in general, be reported to the police or relevant authorities sooner rather than later. These would include stealing from the church, actual bodily harm inflicted on an individual, bigamy or damage to church property. Where such things are told in private confidences, the individual concerned should be encouraged to confess them appropriately, and make whatever restitution is acceptable to all parties, as well as complying with the law. Where ministers and church leaders feel that it is necessary to share a confidence with the church leadership team as a whole, it is vital that the leadership is unanimous in agreeing to keep absolute confidentiality, which should exclude sharing information with spouses.

Each denomination has, or is drawing up, procedures or standing orders to deal with these matters. You should check what your denomination requires.

LEGAL MATTERS

At another level, there are matters which may call for legal advice or action. These would include professional misconduct on the part of a caretaker or other church employee, or the need to evict someone from church premises. It is important to ensure that legal advice is taken in such matters, so that the church is clear about its own responsibilities and liabilities, and can be advised about appropriate action. However, it is always better to reach agreements with the individuals involved where possible, taking legal action only as the last resort.

Consult with your buildings' trustees about matters of employment contracts and property and accommodation. Some denominations have their own standard contracts. If legal action has to be taken, always use a qualified solicitor, preferably someone who specialises in the field concerned. Where the dismissal of an employee is involved, ensure that you fulfil all the necessary procedures for dismissal, or you may find yourself taken to court by your employee. These procedures can be found in Appendix D.

Where potentially legal matters can be dealt with pastorally, and in lesser matters of unacceptable behaviour, the pattern of response suggested by the words of Jesus in Matthew 18:15-17 might be helpfully elaborated as follows:

1. Recognise the problem: minister, leadership team or church meeting decide that the behaviour of an individual or group of people needs serious consideration.

2. Accept responsibility: minister, leadership team or church meeting recognise their responsibility to decide on an appropriate response, even if that is to do nothing.

3. Formulate a response: confront the individual or group privately at first if that is appropriate, with a small group if the response is considered inadequate, and publicly in the church meeting if that second level of encounter does not resolve the situation. Do not make pre-judgements about the truth of allegations, but be ready to approach accused people with an open mind.

4. Carry out the agreed response. (Do not involve the victim of behaviour in a confrontation with the alleged perpetrator.)

5. Discuss with each party concerned how the behaviour, and issues behind it, may be resolved.

ANTISOCIAL BEHAVIOUR

Clearly, different levels of response will be employed with different levels of behaviour. For instance, if a church member wrongly questions the truthfulness of another member's statements in a church meeting, it may be appropriate to challenge that person directly to apologise and withdraw the accusation. Or it may be better to speak to them privately after the meeting and ask them to apologise in person to the individual concerned, and possibly ask them to apologise publicly at a later time – these will be matters of individual judgement, though it may be good to discuss the principles concerned at Church Council or PCC meetings.

Another example would be the church member who is very active in the church, but who tends to give offence to many people, especially newcomers. If s/he is nominated for a leadership role, it may be the judgement of the leadership team that it is inappropriate for him/her to stand. A private word of dissuasion may save public embarrassment or humiliation at the time of an election, if the leadership team would be unwilling to accept a majority vote in the church meeting.

SEXUAL RELATIONSHIPS

Another, and quite different level of behaviour which may cause offence in churches is in the area of sexual relationships. It is now a common situation that marriages between church members break up, and in some cases one or both of the partners, before or after a divorce, may become romantically or sexually involved with another church member. Husbands or wives may be suspected of mentally or physically abusing their partners. Young people enter into sexual relationships which may be publicly acknowledged or not, but which cause offence or concern to their parents or their contemporaries. Gay and lesbian couples may openly acknowledge their relationships and find that these are not welcomed or accepted by other church members. Or it may become clear that a church member is sexually promiscuous.

Such situations are particularly difficult to deal with, because of the complexity of the issues involved, because it is difficult to know how to judge between rival views of the same situation, because whole families may be feeling hurt, and because sexual issues often produce strong emotional reactions among those who are not directly involved.

Consequently, no simple structure for dealing with such situations can be offered, and the model of healing rather than that of justice and retribution, towards which we often tend to gravitate, seems more appropriate. The following are some principles for a healthy approach to such issues. (In Jesus' teaching, to be healthy and to be saved are the same thing.)

- Offer personal support, rather than keeping your distance.
- Do not leap to conclusions; listen carefully to what each person is telling you.
- Resist the temptation to take sides; each person needs support and understanding.
- Recognise that individuals are rarely completely in the right or the wrong.

- Encourage openness, and allow for real differences between people.
- Allow for the strength and irrationality of people's feelings – sometimes hormones take over!
- Identify abuses of power within relationships.
- Recognise that the person who is angriest is not necessarily in the right, or the most abused.
- Remember that faith is about embracing uncertainty, not a set of rules.

Churches differ in what behaviour they find acceptable and what they do not. In practice, matters of principle and justice may influence the outcome less than the feelings generated. The church community may not be able to tolerate the pain of some situations where nobody can be held to blame, and so the people concerned may find that they need to leave, and join another church. In other cases the individuals concerned will be unable to bear the pain, and have to leave, though the community is ready to hold and keep them.

Many of us experience our sexuality as the area in which we find it most difficult to reconcile our principles and our longings as disciples of Christ with the reality of our feelings and our actions. Because of this we may be more careful not to judge others in sexual matters, but equally we may respond in the opposite way by becoming more judgemental in this area than we would be in any other. If individuals and church communities find they have a strong desire to punish people whose sexual behaviour they find unacceptable, it may be important to ask why that is.

THE NEED TO CONFRONT

Churches cannot duck the responsibilities of responding to unacceptable behaviour, of whatever kind it may be, on the part of its members. To do so is to destroy trust, and trust, in God and in each other, is the foundation of a healthy church life. However, Christian love demands that we respond with care and concern for every individual, and with a strong desire to help the person whose behaviour causes offence to understand why. It also demands a constant striving to bring about the reconciliation and forgiveness which are the hallmarks of the Gospel, and of God's continuing work of salvation with each one of us.

Why? It was her! It was it! oopps!

In the beginning was the excuse!

FOR REFLECTION . . .

Reading   John 7:53-8:11

Saying of Jesus   'Let anyone among you who is without sin be the first to throw a stone at her.'
                      (John 8:7)

Reflection   Caught in the Act

Someone caught in the act of breaking a law or social convention embarrasses the Church. Tradition, conventions and laws are broken sometimes unwittingly, sometimes deliberately. Jesus, the Head of the Church, recognises that no-one is so blameless that they can afford to throw the first stone at someone who is caught.

But what should the Church do? The incident of the woman caught in adultery cannot find a permanent resting place in the New Testament. Traditionally it has three different places in the Gospels. It's as if the story is too hot to handle or perhaps, as it reflects a somewhat liberal attitude by Jesus to the woman, the story had difficulty in getting into the canon of scripture.

The Church is always in a dilemma when it tries to exercise its doctrine of love through pastoral care for the individual and its doctrine of justice through executing its disciplinary procedures. Unlike some of the institutions in the world, the doctrines of grace, mercy and forgiveness are essential to the way the Church treats individuals. The sinner is the one who breaks the law, the convention, the standing order. There are degrees of sinning, however. Accusations can be made concerning matters of belief, or sexual matters, or financial management, against any member of the church community, including the minister.

When Jesus asked that awkward question, each individual was in a quandary. Each person probably knew the weaknesses, the peccadilloes of their fellows. Anyone claiming to be faultless would have been subject to the crowd's denial. Even the most experienced knew they were not guiltless. The elders began to leave the scene first. Who was going to administer the punishment to the woman? Jesus was left alone to pass judgement. No doubt the woman recognised Jesus' authority as a Rabbi. She remained and Jesus remained. Sentence had not yet been passed. Those who would condemn have disappeared. Jesus helped the woman to realise and say for herself that no-one had condemned her. And what about the Rabbi? He stated, 'Nor do I condemn you.' This was consistent with the saying in John's Gospel that he had not come to judge the world but to save it (John 3:17).

The Church is always having to protect its image in the world. It not only condemns, it is condemned. It spends time in saving its face. It must make sure its primary role is not to judge but to save. Of course it must investigate when charges are made against its members. But it must be able to exercise mercy and grace as well as justice and not simply protect a pristine image of itself as being blameless.

Sandstone

He bent down and wrote something,
His finger stroking the sand
As if painting
Some word of wisdom
Some abstract doodling
As his mind focused

Perhaps he searched the law
The jot and tittles –
The precedents of judgement
In the Talmud

Sitting upright
Like all the religious
He called the jury
To administer justice –
But they had gone
Alone – she and he,
Even the prying and the curious
Dispersed to home.

He bent again to write
One word perhaps
In the shifting earth
Not set in stone
Forgiveness? Love?
Who knows?

The Founder of the Church
Forgave the sinner
Taken in adultery
Perhaps he wiped the words away
Covered up the sand again
With his hands
Or feet
'You may go,
Sin no more.'

Personal exercise
In silence think of the worst sin you have ever committed.
Have you ever been forgiven?
Who needs to forgive you?

Group exercise
How would you deal with anyone in your church accused of
any of the following list taken from the Ten Commandments?
(Exodus 20)

Accused of/guilty of	Action
taken	
worshipping false gods	
working on the Sabbath	
blasphemy	
swearing	
dishonouring parents	
murder	
adultery	
stealing	
false evidence	
envying or lusting after other people	
envying others' possessions	

How does this list compare with the teaching of Jesus in
Matthew 5: 17-48?

Prayer
Lord, when I am hasty to condemn someone, help me to
pause a while and see who it is I am about to condemn.

APPENDICES

APPENDIX A

Useful reading on methodology and background:

Paul Beasley-Murray, *Power for God's Sake*, Paternoster Press

Tom Douglas, *Basic Groupwork*, Tavistock Publications Ltd

W. R. Bion, *Experiences in Groups*, Tavistock Publications Ltd (the opening section)

Carl R. Rogers, *On Becoming a Person*, Constable

Gerard Egan, *The Skilled Helper*, Brooks/Cole

Patrick Parkinson, *Child Sexual Abuse and the Churches*, Hodder & Stoughton

Steve Shaw, *Dancing with your Shadow*, Triangle SPCK

John Howard Yoder, *Body Politics*, Discipleship Resources, Nashville

Edwin H. Friedman, *Generation to Generation*, The Guilford Press

For the most comprehensive works in this area to date:

Speed B. Leas, *Moving your Church through Conflict*, Alban Institute, N.Y.

Mediation and Facilitation Training Manual: Foundations and Skills for Constructive Conflict Transformation (Third Edition)
Mennonite Conciliation Service, 21 South 12th Street, O.O. Box 500 Akron, PA 17501-0500
(Available through the London Mennonite Centre, 14 Shepherds Hill, Highgate, London N6 5AQ)

Training for Mediation in the Church

Ideally the Mennonite manual should be used in conjunction with the Mennonite Skills Training Course for Mediation in the Church. Details are available from the Mennonite Centre.

APPENDIX B

Self-Perception Exercises

AN EXERCISE TO DISCOVER YOUR PATTERNS OF RESPONSE TO CONFLICT

Patterns of behaviour in responding to conflict and differences of opinion are learned early, and are largely unconscious; there is value in learning what our automatic personal reactions to conflict are likely to be.

Below there are three pairs of possible responses. For each pair, please circle A or B to show which statement is most characteristic of your own behaviour *as it is* (not as you would like it to be, ideally).

If neither A nor B is very close to your typical behaviour, please select the one which is least unlike your probable response. Not all pairs are opposites.

Work through the responses in the order in which the statements occur. The results can then be entered into the Preferred Mode chart which follows.

1. A There are times when I let others take responsibility for solving the problem.
   B Rather than negotiate the things on which we disagree, I try to stress those things on which we both agree.

2. A I try to find a compromise solution.
   B I attempt to deal with all of her/his and my concerns.

3. A I am usually firm in pursuing my goals.
   B I might try to soothe the other's feelings and preserve our relationship.

4. A I try to find a compromise solution.
   B I sometimes sacrifice my own wishes for the wishes of the other person.

5. A I consistently seek the other's help in working out a solution.
   B I try to do what is necessary to avoid useless tensions.

6. A I try to avoid creating unpleasantness for myself.
   B I try to win my position.

7. A I try to postpone the issue until I have had time to think it over.
   B I give up some points in exchange for others.

8. A I am usually firm in pursuing my goals.
   B I attempt to get all concerns and issues immediately out in the open.

9. A I feel that differences are not always worth worrying about.
   B I make some effort to get my way.

10. A I am firm in pursuing my goals.
    B I try to find a compromise solution.

11. A I attempt to get all concerns and issues immediately out in the open.
    B I might try to soothe the other's feelings and preserve our relationship.

12. A I sometimes avoid taking positions which would create controversy.
    B I will sometimes let the other person have some of her/his positions if she/he lets me have some of mine.

13. A I propose a middle ground.
    B I press to get my points made.

14. A I tell the other person my ideas and ask for her/his
    B I try to show the other person the logic and benefits of my choice.

15. A I might try to soothe the other's feelings and preserve our relationship.
    B I try to do what is necessary to avoid tensions.

16 A I try not to hurt the other's feelings.
     B I try to convince the other person of the merits of my position.

17. A I am usually firm in pursuing my goals.
     B I try to do what is necessary to avoid useless tensions.

18. A If it makes other people happy, I might let them maintain their views.
     B I will let other people have some of their positions if they let me have some of mine.

19. A I attempt to get all concerns and issues immediately out in the open.
     B I try to postpone the issue until I have had some time to think it over.

20. A I attempt immediately to work through our differences.
     B I try to find a fair combination of gains and losses for both of us.

21. A In approaching negotiations, I try to be considerate of the other person's wishes.
     B I always lean toward a direct discussion of the problem.

22. A I try to find a position that is intermediate between hers/his and mine.
     B I assert my wishes.

23. A I am very concerned with satisfying all our wishes.
     B There are times when I let others take responsibility for solving the problem.

24. A If the other's position seems very important to her/him, I would try to meet their wishes.
     B I try to get the other person to settle for a compromise.

25. A I try to show the other person the logic and benefits of my position.
     B In approaching negotiations, I try to be considerate of the other person's wishes.

26. A I propose a middle ground.
     B I am nearly always concerned with satisfying all our wishes.

27. A I sometimes avoid taking positions that would create controversy.
    B If it makes other people happy, I might let them maintain their views.

28. A I am usually firm in pursuing my goals.
    B I usually seek the other's help in working out a solution.

29. A I propose a middle ground.
    B I feel that differences are not always worth worrying about.

30. A I try not to hurt the other's feelings.
    B I always share the problem with the other person so that we can work it out.

YOUR PREFERRED MODES

The score card below shows how your preferences indicate your repertoire of conflict modes. The highest score shows the mode you most frequently use; the lowest shows your least preferred mode. This page refers only to YOU; it says nothing about whether your style is effective or appropriate in any situation, and it says nothing about how typical your style is among church people or anyone else.

	Competing (forcing)	Collaborating (problem solving)	Compromising (sharing)	Avoiding (withdrawal)	Accommodating (smoothing)
1.				A	B
2.		B	A		
3.	A				B
4.			A		B
5.		A		B	
6.	B			A	
7.			B	A	
8.	A	B			
9.	B			A	
10.	A		B		
11.		A			B
12.			B	A	
13.	B		A		
14.	B	A			
15.				B	A
16.	B				A
17.	A			B	
18.			B		A
19.		A		B	
20.		A	B		
21.		B			A
22.	B		A		
23.		A		B	
24.			B		A
25.	A				B
26.		B	A		
27.				A	B
28.	A	B			
29.			A	B	
30.		B			A

Add up the number of items circled in each column:

Competing	Collaborating	Compromising	Avoiding	Accommodating
_____	_____	_____	_____	_____

YOUR MODES IN A BROADER CONTEXT

(Statistics from managers at the middle and upper levels of business and government organisations in the U.S.A.)

If you transfer your scores from the previous page to the columns below you will see how you compare with the 'norm': for example, if you score B on competing, you use this style more than 80% of people tested; if you score 8 on accommodating, you use this more than 90%; if you score 8 on collaborating, you are about in the middle.

		Competing	Collaborating	Compromising	Avoiding	Accommodating
	100%	12		12	12	12
					11	11
		11	12	11	10	10
		10	11	10	9	9
	90%					
High 25%		9	10			7
		8		9	8	
	80%					
				9		6
		7		8		
	70%					
					7	
	60%					
		6				
			8			5
				7	6	
Middle 50%	50%					
			7			
		5				
	40%					
						4
				6		
		4			5	
	30%					
			6	5		
						3
Low 25%		3			4	
	20%					
			5			
				4		
		2			3	
	10%					
			4			
			3	3		
			2	2	2	2
		1	1	1	1	1
	0%					

77

CONFLICT MANAGEMENT MODES

P
R
O
D
U
C
T

P E O P L E

Competing: Assertive + uncooperative – pursuing one's own goals at the other's expense.
High on Product; low on People
'I am firm in pursuing my goals.'

Accommodating: Unassertive + cooperative – neglecting one's own concerns to satisfy the other.
High on People; low on Product
'If it makes the other happy, I might let them keep their own views.'

Avoiding: Unassertive + uncooperative – neglecting both one's own and other's concerns by not addressing the issue.
Low on People and Product
'I feel that this is not worth worrying about.'

Collaborating: Assertive + cooperative – digging into an issue to satisfy both parties completely.
High on People and Product
'I tell them my ideas and ask them for theirs.'

Compromising: Intermediate in both assertiveness and cooperation – attempting to satisfy partially both oneself and the other by finding a 'middle-ground'
Middling on People and Product.
'I try to find a fair mix of gains and losses for both of us.'

Mark each of these styles on the grid above. Mark your preferred styles – 1, 2, 3, 4, 5.

RELATING STYLES

(Mark out of a total of 45 for distribution in each column)
How are you most likely to behave with your:

Significant Other		Business Contact		Church Leader	
Sympathise	☐	Sympathise	☐	Sympathise	☐
Negotiate	☐	Negotiate	☐	Negotiate	☐
Yield	☐	Yield	☐	Yield	☐
Compel	☐	Compel	☐	Compel	☐
Persuade	☐	Persuade	☐	Persuade	☐
Support	☐	Support	☐	Support	☐
Total	45		45		45

[The preceding material in Appendix B is The Thomas-Kilmann Conflict Mode Instrument, copyright of: XICOM Inc., Sterling Forest Tuxedo, N.Y 10987 U.S.A.]

Groupwork Self-perception Exercise

A useful description of different ways of operating within groups is described in *Management Teams* by R. Meredith Belbin.

It is possible, if not ideal, to read the description of the eight different styles of involvement in groups which Belbin defines on page 74 without reading the whole book, and then to use the self-perception inventory on pages 148-152.

Conflict intensity Chart
Characteristics

LEVEL 5:	INTRACTABLE
1. Issue	No longer clear understanding of issue; personalities have become the issue. Conflict now unmanageable.
2. Emotions	Relentless obsession in accomplishing the objective(s) at all cost. Vindictive. No objectivity or control of emotion.
3. Orientation	Sees person(s) as harmful to society, not just to offended group or person.
4. Information	Information skewed to accomplish the objective at any cost.
5. Language	Focuses on words that imply the destruction and/or elimination of the other.
6. Objective	To destroy the offending party/persons; eg to see that the 'sacked' pastor does not get a call elsewhere.
7. Outcome	Highly destructive. Use of compulsion to maintain peace. May be necessary to remove members from church. Possible formation of 'commission of enquiry'.

LEVEL FOUR:	FIGHT/FLIGHT
1. Issue	Shifts from winning to getting rid of person(s). No longer believe others can change, or want them to change.
2. Emotions	Cold self-righteousness. Will not speak to the other side.
3. Orientation	Factions are solidified. Clear lines of demarcation. Last place for *constructive* intervention by third party consultant.
4. Information	Limited only to the cause being advocated; will not listen to or accept contrary information.
5. Language	Talk is now of 'principles', not issues. Language solidifies into ideology.
6. Objective	No longer just winning; now means eliminating other(s) from the environment. Hurt the other.
7. Outcome	High probability of split within the church with significant numbers leaving the church.

LEVEL THREE: CONTEST

1. Issue   Begins the dynamics of WIN/LOSE. Resistance to peace overtures. Focus on persons representing the enemy.

2. Emotions   Not able to operate in the presence of the 'enemy'; however, can admire a worthy opponent. Not willing/able to share emotions/feeling constructively.

3. Orientation Personal attacks. Formation of factions/sides. Threats of members leaving. Need third party consultant from outside.

4. Information Distortion is major problem. Information shared only within faction.

5. Language   Overgeneralisation: 'You always ...' 'We never ...' Attribute diabolical motives to others.

6. Objective   Shifts from self-protection to winning. Objectives are more complex and diffuse; issues are clustered.

7. Outcome   Decision-making – mediation, compromising, voting. Possible that some will leave the church when the decision 'goes the wrong way'.

LEVEL TWO: DISAGREEMENT

1. Issue   Real disagreement; mixing of personalities and issues; problems cannot be clearly defined.

2. Emotions   Distrust beginning. Caution in association, less mixing with 'the other side'.

3. Orientation Begin personalising problem; shrewdness and calculation begin.

4. Information Selective hold-back of information occurs on both sides.

5. Language   More vague and general; 'Some people ...' 'They ...': hostile humour, barbed comment and put-down.

6. Objective   Face-saving; come out looking good. Tend to move towards consensus. Not yet win/lose conflict.

7. Outcome   Attempt collaborative solution or negotiate acceptable agreement; win/win with real effort.

LEVEL ONE: PROBLEM TO SOLVE

1. Issue — Real disagreement; conflicting goals, values, needs, etc.

2. Emotions — Short-lived anger, quickly controlled; parties begin to be uncomfortable in the presence of other(s).

3. Orientation — Tends to be problem orientated rather than personalised.

4. Information — Open sharing of information.

5. Language — Clear and specific.

6. Objective — Solving the problem. Move towards unanimous agreement. Utilise collaborative styles.

7. Outcome — Collaborative agreement if possible. Win/win resolution with acceptable, mutually agreed solution.

This chart was originally produced by the Task Force on Pastor/ Congregation Conflict of the Alban Institute, USA.

APPENDIX C

Outline of team-building exercise with a leadership team

Obtain agreement to the process, which will involve working as a group to examine group aims and objectives, and discuss the hopes and fears of those involved in the group about the group itself.

Deal with any immediate issues, like people absenting themselves.

FIRST MEETING

EXERCISE 1. What is this group for? [Materials: blank 2 by 4 cards, flip-chart]

a) Brainstorm all possible aims for this group, and record them on a board.

b) Copy each reason onto two cards.

c) Shuffle the cards and share them equally between the members of the group.

d) Members trade cards to acquire the ones expressing their main aims.

e) After trading, sit in circle and discuss whether they have the cards they want.

f) Record on the original list those aims which predominate, and add any that need adding.

EXERCISE 2. Things I do badly [Materials: none]

a) In a circle each person has a turn saying the thing they do most badly.

b) The next round everyone says the thing people tell them they do well. (People say . . .)

c) The third round everyone says the thing they know they do well.

d) Discuss how it felt to say these things.

EXERCISE 3. Fear in a hat [Materials: paper, pencils, basket]

a)   Each person, in a circle, anonymously completes on paper the sentence 'In this leadership team I am afraid that . . .

b)   The pieces of paper are put in the basket and handed round. Each person takes one, reads it, and enlarges on the sentence to try to express what the person was feeling.

c)   No arguing or comment is allowed.

d)   After every sentence has been read, discuss what was noticed or discovered.

SECOND MEETING

1.   Spend a short time reflecting on the previous meeting, and ask for any thoughts on it, or subsequent reactions to it.

2.   Ask if anybody has a particular matter or approach they want to bring to this meeting.

3.   Seek agreement on the subject-matter of the meeting.

EXERCISE 1. (Use flipchart)

a)   Make a list of current 'issues' about which group members are, or might be, divided.

b)   Choose the one that seems to have the most energy and involvement associated with it.

c)   Tease out the different issues and attitudes which contribute to it. What difficulties prevent the issues from being resolved satisfactorily?

EXERCISE 2. (If there is time: otherwise propose this for a subsequent meeting)

Choose one or more of the aims of the leadership team agreed at the previous meeting, and discuss what the team needs to do to implement that aim or those aims.

THIRD MEETING

EXERCISE 1. (Use flipchart)

Draw up a mission statement, or covenant, for the leadership group that all can agree with and put into effect. Discuss the implications of this for the church as a whole, and what needs to be communicated to the church about this process.

Ensure that the subjects of confidentiality, group responsibility, abiding by group decisions, the role of the minister, and others that have emerged as issues, are fully examined, and any necessary action agreed.

APPENDIX D

Legal requirements in the case of dismissal of an employee

Stage 1: Formal oral warning

Keep a record of the date, time and place, and the fact that the warning was given.

Examples of misconduct which may lead to a formal warning include:

- Absence without permission
- Poor timekeeping
- Failure to report damage to church property as soon as possible
- Failure to carry out duties adequately
- Poor work performance
- Improper use of the church's equipment
- Failure to observe reasonable standards of behaviour

Stage 2: Written warning

Either as a follow-up to the oral warning where this has not achieved a satisfactory change, or if the matter is of a more serious nature. The warning should be given verbally, confirmed in writing, and include:

- The nature of the complaint
- The required standards that must be met
- If appropriate, a time limit for improvement
- A note that further disciplinary action will result if the required standards are not met, or if there is further misconduct
- A note of the right to appeal, and how and where this should be made

Examples of misconduct which lead to a written warning might include:

- Refusal or failure to obey a legitimate instruction
- Actions likely to bring the church into disrepute
- Repetition of misconduct or behaviour which led to the oral warning being issued

Stage 3: Final written warning

This should include the same information as the first three items of Stage 2, plus a warning that the employee will be dismissed if the standards are not met or there is further misconduct. The right of appeal should again be offered.

Stage 4: Dismissal

This should be confirmed in writing, with details of an appeals procedure.

Gross Misconduct

Certain issues might be so serious as to warrant summary dismissal without prior warning. Legal advice should be sought beforehand. Examples of gross misconduct could include:

- Criminal acts
- Sexual or racial harassment or discrimination
- Deception, especially in financial matters and sickness/absence
- Negligence
- Persistent refusal or failure to obey a legitimate instruction
- Assault
- Indecent or immoral acts
- Being under the influence of alcohol or narcotic drugs whilst on duty

Acknowledgements

Scripture quotations, unless otherwise stated, are from the New Revised Standard Version of the Bible, copyright 1989 by the Division of Christian Education of the National Council of the Churches of Christ in the USA.

p. 14, 71   Carl R. Rogers, *On Becoming a Person,* Constable & Robinson Publishing Ltd.

p. 79   The Thomas-Kilmann Conflict Mode Instrument, XICOM Inc. Permission applied for.

p.79-82   Task Force on Pastor/Congregation Conflict of The Alban Institute, USA. Permission applied for.

Material in Chapter Nine has been adapted from a paper prepared by the Thames North Province's team of Pastoral Consultants on behalf of the Mission Council of the United Reformed Church in the United Kingdom, 1998

Cartoons by Brian Wigglesworth.

Front Cover design by Martin Eggleton.